The Instructional Design and Development Process: A 'How To' Guide for Practitioners

Instructional Design

Ray Pastore, Ph.D.

1st Edition

About this Text

Do you want to know 'how to do' Instructional Design? Are you trying to design or develop training? Are you developing eLearning? Are you interested in the field and want to learn more? The following text is based on Dr. Ray Pastore's Instructional Design Video Series and is designed to teach you 'how to' be an instructional designer.

This text is based on Dr. Ray Pastore's Instructional Design Video Series. Captions from each of the videos were transcribed and then organized for this text. As a result, the language of this text might feel less formal than my research papers!

About the Author

Dr. Ray Pastore has extensive corporate, government, K-12, and higher education experience. With a background in management consulting and instructional design, he earned his Ph.D. in Instructional Systems including a minor in Educational Psychology from Penn State University in 2008 and is currently an Associate Professor and Program Coordinator of the Instructional Technology master's program as well as Esports Club Advisor at the University of North Carolina Wilmington. He has worked on projects for Fortune 500 companies, the US Department of Defense, as well as a myriad of schools and universities. He also runs a technology Youtube channel which has several million views.

Research: Dr. Pastore's research focuses on multiple representations (multimedia), gaming and esports, mobile learning, and metacognitive strategies that support learning from a multimedia environment.

Teaching: Dr. Pastore has been teaching face-to-face, online, and hybrid courses for many years. He has taught at Penn State University, Slippery Rock University, Walden University, the University of Phoenix, and most recently the University of North Carolina Wilmington. His teaching experience includes a wide variety of courses on topics including: technology use in the K-16 classroom and corporate workplace, instructional design practice and theory, project management, online course design and development, programming, gaming, esports, virtual reality, mobile learning, and multimedia development (CBT).

Personal: I would just say Dr. Pastore lives in Wilmington, NC with his wife and three sons, or wife and family. In his free time he enjoys surfing, Brazilian Jiu Jitsu (Purple Belt), golfing, painting, gaming, and spending time with his family.

Contact

Website, contact, and links for Youtube ID video series: http://raypastore.com/

Special Thanks

Thanks to Jean Lohmann for editing this text. It was a difficult process due to the nature of its design.

ISBN 9798651489978

Publisher KDP

Date 2020

Edition 1

Citing this text:

Pastore, R. (2020). *The Instructional Design and Development Process: A 'How To' Guide for Practitioners.* Kindle Direct Publishing.

Table of Contents

Introduction

1.0 What is Instructional Design (ID)? – p. 7

Before You Begin

2.0 Front End Analysis – p. 15

3.0 The Many ID Models – p. 22

Analysis

4.0 Needs Analysis and Needs Assessment – p. 24

4.1 Task Analysis – p. 36

Design

5.0 Learning Objectives – p. 45

5.1 Instructional Congruency – p. 51

5.2 Assessments – p. 52

5.3 Instructional Strategies – p. 63

Development

6.0 Common Deliverables – p. 71

6.1 Prototyping and Storyboards – p. 76

6.2 Style Guide – p. 81

6.3 Software IDs Use – p. 84

6.4 Theories behind Multimedia Development – p. 89

6.5 Multimedia Development – p. 92

6.6 Usability – p. 95

6.7 Pilot Testing – p. 97

Implementation

7.0 Implementation – p. 99

Evaluation

8.0 Evaluation – p. 102

Beyond Traditional ID

9.0 Rapid ID: What, When, and How - p. 106

References

10.0 References - p. 110

1.0 What is Instructional Design (ID)?

Are you wondering what an Instructional Designer (ID) does? Are you considering trying to become an ID? Maybe you are hiring an ID and/or need to write a job description. Maybe you want to explain to a relative what exactly you do. Well, it would be convenient if there was an easy way to explain it. Numerous definitions of the field appear in many sources including books, organizations, journals, presentations, the web, etc. But guess what? It's very difficult to explain because we can do so many different things and fulfill multiple job roles.

For example, some might consider an ID someone that simply develops eLearning courses or someone that only writes assessments. In part, they are correct, these are SOME of the things an ID is able to do but that isn't all - not even close. That would be similar to thinking a mechanic only does oil changes. ID is much more than just developing eLearning. As a result, the following section will describe, at a very basic (high) level, what an ID does and the rest of the sections in this text will be spent going into the minute details of everything explained here!

At the most basic level, instructional design can be described as a systematic process used to develop instruction in order to improve learner achievement of a learning objective that is measured through some form of assessment (Dick, Carey, and Carey, 2014). That is a very high-level description of what one needs to be able to do to be an instructional designer - but all of the steps of going from point A to point Z are missing from that definition and there are a lot of them!

Having said that, our field is all of this and so much more, and IDs are expected to be able to be capable of even more. If you were to browse through job descriptions in the ID field you would see they barely mention what is described in this definition, in fact, you would probably notice each one is vastly different from one another - some looking for a developer, some looking for an evaluation expert, others looking for an LMS administrator, etc.

What do we really do? How can we do all of these different jobs? As an ID, you should be able to fill multiple roles, for example, assess a situation through analysis, determine solutions, conduct needs analysis, create learning objectives, design instruction, design assessments, develop instruction, train trainers, train learners, develop materials for instruction, implement training, evaluate training, manage training projects, and write training proposals. This is far from an exhaustive list - I could probably add hundreds of additional tasks. And I should note that some IDs focus or specialize on only one or some of these while others are a jack of all trades. The best way to start describing ID is by explaining the ID process, which will give you a clearer picture of what an ID can do.

The following image (Figure 1.0) depicts the instructional process from start to finish:

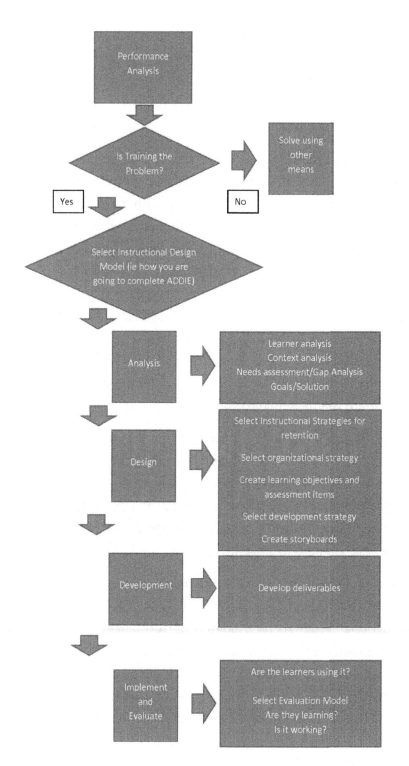

9

This is an image of the Instructional process from start to finish
The selected model is only linear in this image to show the learner how the process works from start to finish. This does not imply that the instructional process is actually linear or the model you choose will be.

Ideally, the ID process has a clear start and end though this will vary by project. Before instructional design happens, we (we as in instructional designers) are presented with a problem. This problem can come from many different places - the client, an analysis, new software, a lawsuit, a new law, a proposal, and so on. Once there is a problem, the first step is to conduct a performance analysis. This performance analysis is where we figure out what the problem really is, the cause of the problem, and what interventions (solutions) we can use to solve the problem. As an ID, the problem is either solved through training, where we then solve it, or non-training, where we work with the appropriate team/people to solve it.

If a training solution does not solve the problem, then we solve the problem through other means. That might involve fixing an error on a website or database, communicating a message, motivating employees with more money, or a more flexible work schedule. Whatever the intervention to the non-training problem is, we help to solve it.

If a training solution does solve the problem, we then truly begin the instructional design process. Thus, it is imperative that instructional designers be trained in performance improvement/performance analysis. You must be able to ensure that training is the solution to the problem you are solving. Otherwise, you might be working on a solution that will not solve the problem and that could be catastrophic for your client or even your career. You could be blamed or even worse, possibly fired for not solving the correct problem with the correct solution even though you might have been listening to your boss or client. Remember, you are the one that needs to make sure the problem and cause are correctly identified before starting a new project.

However, once we have a training problem/solution we can then move into the ID process. At this point, we need to figure out which ID model will work best given our current case. There are thousands of models out there, each being a variation of what's called the "ADDIE Framework" (see section 3.0 of text for more on ADDIE). I am not going to cover the 1000 different variations of ADDIE that exist, but rather go through a basic version of the ADDIE framework in this text, which I will stress throughout this book, **should be modified for every single project!**

What model should we choose? Are we going to use Dick and Carey's (Dick, Carey, Carey, 2014), which is a very popular model? What about Smith and Ragan's (Smith and Ragan, 2004)? What about a rapid design model? What are we going to choose? **We choose the model that best helps us solve the problem.** Once we've selected our model, we're going to modify it as needed for our project.

Take a very good look at the image in this section, Figure 1.0, showing the high-level depiction of ADDIE so that you can see how a basic ID process could work. After we have done our front-end/performance analysis, we have our instructional needs analysis. This is where we're going to identify learner needs, project needs, the content, identify the gaps, and come up with project goals and solutions. This is the stage where I usually write a proposal for a client so that I can begin design and development of the project...and get paid!

Once that analysis is complete and we have approval from our client/sponsor to move forward, we can begin to design. This is where we design whatever we stated would solve our problem. This is where we decide how to organize the instruction. Thus, we choose an organizational strategy (i.e., Gagne's 9 Events) for the type of instructional we are going to develop (i.e. eLearning, instructor-led, etc.). The organizational strategy is designed to make sure your instruction is organized, for example, have your objectives first, then present your content, then have some kind of assessment and feedback. It is also during this process that we create our learning objectives and assessments.

Additionally, during design, we have to select our instructional strategies for retention. Instructional strategies are what helps the learners learn. For example, think of an activity you did as a student at some point during your education when a teacher was presenting content such as a worksheet, case study, game, explaining concepts, etc. Those are examples of instructional strategies. We're going to put those into our instruction to make it so that our learners learn. At the end of design all of our content should be organized so that we can begin to develop!

Next, we move into development. We need to develop whatever materials are required for our project, whether that's computer-based instruction (eLearning), web-based instruction, an instructor-led course, a game, or a simulation. We develop the deliverables. Unfortunately, some people believe this development phase is all an ID does. They assume we just develop eLearning. As you can see this is only one part of what an ID does and it doesn't stop here!

Now we're going to implement it, roll it out, and/or give it to the client for actual use. This is where you hand the project off to the client and it goes live, you teach the course, you train the trainers, you install the software, etc. Depending on the requirements of the project, implementation can be as simple as handing a project to a client or as complicated as you conducting the training yourself!

Finally, Evaluation. We conduct formative evaluation (checks and balances for quality) throughout the whole ID process. However, we also evaluate the overall effectiveness of our training solution. For this final summative evaluation, we select an evaluation model (i.e., Kirkpatrick's model). This is where we determine if the learners learned, if they enjoyed the training, if it's being applied to their job, if it solved the problem, and the return on investment. Depending on the project goals, evaluation may take place during training roll out or at a much later time (months or years later). In general, not all companies/organizations invest in evaluation but it is a vital step in the process.

There you have it folks, that's the quick and dirty overview of the entire instructional design process and explains "some" of the things an ID could do as part of their job. Having said that, there's a lot more to each of these steps and I will go into more depth in each of the following sections. Keep in mind one of the things that I find that new IDs have a lot of problems with, even towards the end of a master's program, is the big picture. This section was the big picture. This is how it all fits together. It's not complicated, and sometimes we make it more complicated than it really needs to be. I would recommend reading this section again once you have read through all of the other sections in this text, it will really help you put the complete picture together.

2.0 Front End Analysis

Front End Analysis (FEA) (also referred to as performance analysis and performance improvement depending on who you are talking to) happens before the instructional design process and is something an ID is expected to be able to do. As an instructional designer, you should understand what this is before you start the instructional design process because it's something that's always going to be done in an organization to make sure that you're actually solving the problem and that the problem is the correct one (yes sometimes you won't be solving a problem at all but we will get to that later!).

Why do you do this performance analysis? What is it? What is the purpose? We do this to determine what the problem is and then to figure out the appropriate intervention (solution). Is this a training problem? Is this a communication problem? Is there a glitch in the computer system? Is this a motivation problem? Are there multiple problems?

Many times a client will come to the instructional designer with a problem and possible solution. However, we can't always take their word for it (though sometimes we have no choice). We do not know if they have correctly identified the problem, root cause, and solution. Thus, we must do a front-end analysis to determine if they are correct. Ideally in a perfect world, we have as much time as needed to conduct a thorough front-end analysis but in practice that is not the case. Time is limited. Sometimes this means I get a (as in one) phone call with a client and that's it!

How do we begin a front-end analysis? How do we figure out what the problem is? Many times, the client's going to come to us and tell us they have the problem and tell us how they want it solved - this is my experience most of the time. Usually what they want at this point is confirmation that their solution will work and they want me to nod my head and say 'OK'. However, you always need to go in knowing that you need to find the problem and cause then worry about the solution. So...

What I want to do here in this section is to explain the ideal way to do this front-end analysis but please understand that realistically you may never be able to go through this entire process - it's going to depend on the project. My advice is to learn the proper way first and then learn how and when you can cut corners. The first thing you need to do, especially when starting out, is to select a front-end or performance analysis model. This model will help guide you through the process to find the problem. Following a model helps ensure quality and project success.

Here is a sample model (Figure 2.0) that I use. Keep in mind that the model is going to change based on the project. This is a model that can, should, and needs to be adjusted for every single project. The idea is to look at it and take what is needed for the current situation. As I mentioned previously, sometimes I need to figure out the problem, cause, and solution in one phone call! Knowing what information you need and knowing what questions you need to ask is vital to project success!

Figure 2.0 – Front-end Analysis Model

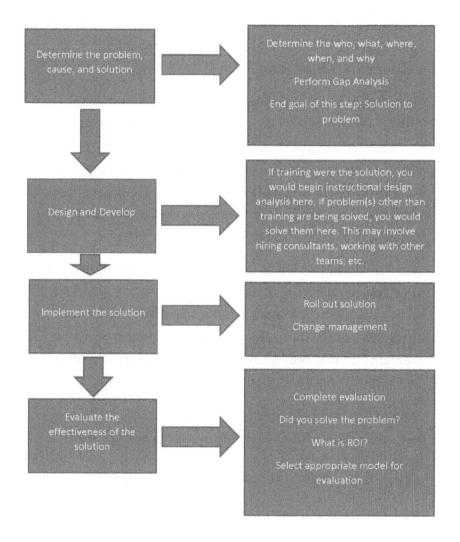

The first step in this model is to determine the problem. What is the problem? This is the *who what, where, and when.* In order to do that, I need to determine who the client is. Who are the stakeholders? What are their needs? What is their organization/infrastructure like?

How do we get this information? It can come from many different sources. Interviews, meetings, observations, surveys, document analysis, etc. It's really different for every project. Most of the time, it's a meeting or two with a manager and subject matter expert (SME). That's it. After those 1-2 meetings, I am able to write a proposal for them with a solution to their problem. It is not the ideal next step, but it's reality.

Next, we determine what the cause of the problem really is? How do you determine the root cause of the problem? We don't want to just look at the actual symptoms. We want to look for the actual cause. There are many ways to do this, fishbone diagrams, charts, brainstorming, data gathering, etc. Which method you choose is up to you.

One way to find the cause that I particularly like is the 'why' exercise (Olivier, 2017). The idea is to keep asking "why" multiple times until we come up with a cause. It's really simple and works to find the cause for many types of problems.

For example, if you were a mechanic, a client might come to you and say 'we need to fix my car, it's dented'. That is a simple temporary solution but as an ID, we don't just want to solve the immediate problem, we want to ensure it doesn't happen again. Thus, we need to find the cause of this problem to prevent it from happening again. So we ask 'why?'.

Me: *Why?* **Client:** *Because another car must have hit/scratch it.*

Me: *Why?* **Client:** *Because it was parked on a narrow street.*

Me: *Why?* **Client:** *Because I didn't want to park it in the driveway.*

Me: *Why?* **Client:** *Because there were two other cars in my driveway.*

Me: *Why?* **Client:** *Because I haven't cleaned my garage. So my other cars can't fit in the garage.*

So now we have the root cause of the problem. Why did the car get damaged? The symptom was the damage from parking on a narrow street which I can't control but we can control where they park it. The reason it was parked in a bad spot was because the garage was not clean. I got to the root cause by asking why, why, why. The solution to this problem is a clean garage and this problem will no longer happen.

Once we have identified the problem(s) and cause, it's time to figure out a solution, so we do a gap analysis. Even if the solution is obvious we should still do the gap analysis to ensure we solve the problem correctly. And if there are multiple problems/causes, it may be impossible to solve all of them so we can rank and prioritize them if needed. I like to do this by asking 'how important is this problem' and 'what is the impact of solving/not solving it'. Once we rank order and determine solutions for each we will need to decide if there is enough time and resources to solve each one.

How do we perform the gap analysis? We look at 3 pieces of information: current state, desired state, and recommended solutions. See table 1.0:

Table 1.0

Current State	Desired State	Recommended
What is the current state of the problem?	What does the client desire?	What is the optimal solution that meets the clients needs?

The current state refers to the current state that led to the problem. What is currently happening? The desired state are the effects of fixing the problem. What does the client desire? Sometimes the client's desires are not possible, which is why we recommend a solution. The recommended solution is the solution that we can do in time/budget. If the clients desired state is not possible the solution needs to describe why.

I may need to present the client with multiple solutions so that they can decide what they need. When doing this I make sure I give them the return on investment (ROI) of each potential solution. This includes telling them how much it will cost, what resources are needed, how long it will take, and impacts. At this point, we need to agree upon a solution with the client. Usually, a statement of work with budget, schedule, and project plan are created at this point.

Once we've identified our problem and we've come up with some solutions for it with our client, we are ready to start on our interventions (solutions). What does that mean? That means if training was the problem, we use an ID model and begin the design and development process (see section 3.0). Otherwise, we solve it with other means, for example, if it was a communication issue, we deal with the communication issue (hopefully with communication experts but sometimes as an ID we need to fill that role too). Then we implement those solutions. If there's change in the organization, we may be implementing some change strategies.

Now, assuming you have completed the front-end analysis and there is a training need, we begin the ID process.

3.0 The Many ID Models

Before we dive into ID, we must first consider an ID model to guide our design and development. Thus, a discussion on the infamous ADDIE framework is needed.

ADDIE is the thing we love to hate and you will hear a lot about it as an ID. Some of what you hear will be correct but unfortunately, some will not. What is ADDIE? ADDIE is a framework that instructional designers use to design and deliver training. You will hear it referred to as the ADDIE Model, ADDIE Framework, etc. with many different definitions of what that means depending on who you are talking to. There has been a lot of misinformation about ADDIE posted in texts, on the internet, and through word of mouth in recent years. Even trusted sources have posted misinformation! So what exactly does ADDIE stand for? Can I use it? Can I modify it? Can I replace it? What model should I be using?

ADDIE is an acronym that stands for Analysis, Design, Development, Implementation, and Evaluation. It was first developed in the 1970s at Florida State for the military and was a linear model used to guide the design and development of instruction (Branson et al., 1975). However, after a few years of testing, it was realized that the linear model originally proposed didn't work so well in practice so it was modified to be more dynamic, less structured, and as a template that could be modified for a particular use.

How we perform each step of that framework varies by project, company, and client which has led to a myriad of ID models. **There are many different ways to perform each step of ADDIE.**

Again, there is no set standard that tells us that we have to perform step 1 (analysis) a certain way. Instead, the way we perform analysis should be the way that best matches the project we are on. This is why you hear of so many different instructional design models - each is trying to prescribe the 'best' way to perform that analysis (or design, or development, etc.). However, there is NO best model that works for everything. The best model is the one that solves your current problem.

ADDIE as a framework does not define how to complete the process of analysis, design, development, implementation, and evaluation. There are many different processes and models out there that define how we should do an analysis. In fact, an analysis will change for every single project you're on because clients have different needs. For some projects, the analysis might be given to you, you might only have a one-hour meeting to conduct it, or you might have weeks to conduct a very thorough analysis; the point being that it's going to differ for every project. This is why as an instructional designer you should know multiple ways to perform each of these steps. Thus, know many different models. When you meet with your client you will recommend a model after you hear what they want to do. You don't recommend a model before hearing their problem, budget, timeframe, etc. You can't say, our company uses XYZ model because your client may need you to use a different one.

Essentially this means that there are numerous different ways to do an analysis, design, development, etc. And sometimes you can perform some of these steps at the same time. Sometimes you need to work in a very linear fashion. This is why you see many different instructional design models out there. As you become a more advanced instructional designer, you will determine your own preferences, what works for you, what works for your clients, and what works for your projects.

When you're first starting out, my recommendation is to try to follow a concise linear process to understand how to do each of the steps. This way you learn to do the steps properly so that you can learn to modify them as you become more experienced. But be aware that's not how you will really always do it. Regardless of what model you're following, they're all following the ADDIE framework. ADDIE is the basic building block, the framework for all of these. Regardless of the model being used, it's using ADDIE as its framework. Thus, you cannot replace ADDIE and if you hear someone talking about replacing ADDIE with X model, be wary of the snake oil they are selling. You can however modify each step of ADDIE for your project so that the process works for your client. Hopefully, that helps you have a better understanding of what that term is. But that's all ADDIE is - analysis, design, development, implementation, and evaluation. Now that the discussion of ADDIE is out of the way, let's discuss the nuts and bolts of ID!

Analysis

4.0 Needs Analysis and Assessment

Once performance analysis (front-end analysis) is completed (the problem, cause, and solutions identified), we are ready to begin the 'formal' instructional design process. As described earlier, we begin with an instructional needs analysis and needs assessment. **Most often (in practice), I've done the front-end analysis and needs analysis/assessment at the same time, so what is being discussed here isn't necessarily in a specific order, rather, you need to do this whether it's done during front-end analysis or after.** Just be aware that you need to gather this information and usually this is all done together at the same time.

The goal of the instructional analysis and needs assessment is to determine the best way to solve the training problem identified in the front-end analysis. But wait, didn't we determine the solution in the front-end analysis? Not necessarily! The front-end analysis determined that training was the solution to the problem. It did not tell us how to solve the training problem (i.e., instructor-led training, computer-based training, mobile learning, etc.). The training needs analysis does this. I know this can sound confusing and it is because I am trying to separate two things that are usually done in unison so that you can see the differences. This is why I stress - I do these at the same time In practice.

In a perfect world, I spend a significant amount of time with my client, the users, and their system/content to do a thorough analysis. However, in many cases, I am working in the role of the consultant and I gather this information in one to several meetings with my client as described in the front-end analysis section. Knowing this, I come prepared to my initial meetings ready to gather a ton of information. Why? Because usually when I am in the role of the consultant, rather than a full-time employee, I am doing this analysis before I have a contract - Why? Because I must do the analysis to come up with a solution so that I can estimate a budget/schedule.

Remember the point of performance/front-end analysis is to determine if training is really the problem and the point of an instructional analysis is to determine what training solution is best. Once I have this information, I can then write up a proposal that the client agrees upon. Once I have the proposal signed, I start doing the design and getting compensation. Thus, many times I am doing this analysis gratis hoping to win a contract. That's just the way the game is played. Having said that, there are times the client pays me before I do any kind of analysis. When that happens I make sure I charge an hourly rate vs. a fixed rate. Additionally, if I am a full-time employee at a company, I may not need to write a proposal but I will still usually write a plan to get approved before I start a project. Keep in mind all of this will vary based on where you work!

That is the what, now onto the doing! How do you do a needs analysis and needs assessment? What is the difference between a needs analysis and needs assessment?

Training Charter

As an instructional designer, one of the first things I like to do when I am starting a project is to create a training charter. I start this on day 1 during my first client communication. The training charter is designed to outline all of the basic project information and will continue to be populated as I complete my analysis. This is very similar to a business plan. Why do we do this? This is done so that I have an organized document containing all of the project details (this is similar to a project charter that a Project Manager (PM) would create).

This charter should contain the information from your front-end analysis (if one was completed).

Example data I include in this charter:

- Who is the client?

- What is the problem?

- What was the cause of the problem?

- How are we solving this problem (what interventions)?

- Who are the people working on this project/stakeholders?

- Who are the managers?

- Who are the Subject Matter Experts (SMEs)?

- What's the return on investment of solving it?

- Do we have a budget?

- Do we have a schedule?

- What other information is important?

Wait, isn't this the stuff the project manager (PM) should be doing? This is where the lines between a PM and ID become blurred. You may need to fulfill both roles here - even if you have a PM. Additionally, there are times where some of this information is withheld, or simply not given to the instructional designer even though we are tasked with designing a solution to the problem because no one realizes we need it. As a result, this charter is a must so that the PM and Subject Matter Experts (SMEs) know we need this information if we are to design and develop some type of training. If we are having problems getting any of this information, it becomes really difficult to come up with a good solution, which is why good analysis is so important. Good analysis helps ensure quality; bad analysis ensures poor quality (not meeting client's objectives).

Now, if you're an internal instructional designer or continuing work for a client, you may know a lot of the analysis already because you've already done most of the up-front work before. You know who your client/customer/sponsor is and you know the problem, so you may be able to skip a lot of this because it would just be rework to do it again. So keep in mind, I'm talking to the person who doesn't have anything, starting from scratch - and that is how you should learn. To recap, the first part of an instructional design project that I create should be coming up with a basic ID project charter.

Sometimes we are told how to design/develop the training from the client, so a needs analysis and needs assessment is a rather short process (i.e. one meeting). Sometimes we have done the instructional analysis/assessment during the front-end analysis. Other times we are just brought into the process at this point. Either way, we want to do an instructional analysis. This will help us go from a training solution to a more detailed approach. For example, we know that training is the problem but is it computer-based training? Classroom-based? Do they have or need for a learning management system? Are these adult learners? Kids? Etc. We need to come up with a detailed solution to the training need so that we can appropriately design and develop training that will meet everyone's needs. We can't design before we know this information. The worst thing that can happen is project failure. For example, if you just listen to the client that says they want five one-hour modules and agree upon a price, finally get the content and realize it's going to be 10 hourly modules. They may fire you for not recommending this from the start. I've seen situations like this happen because the client doesn't know. You are the expert, so it's on you. No matter what happened in that situation, it's your fault and you look bad. This is why good analysis can make or break the project.

Needs Analysis and Needs Assessment

Once we have created a basic charter, it's time to do a needs analysis. The needs analysis is a combination of the learner analysis, context analysis, and gap analysis. The needs assessment, often discussed in ID and often used interchangeably with needs analysis is simply the needs of the client identified during the gap analysis. In addition to that, I usually do a very brief content analysis here as well. Each of these steps is done at the exact same time.

Learner Analysis. The learner analysis seeks to determine who the learners are that are going to be going through your training. For example, you are going to try to determine: Who are the learners? What is their level of education? Can they use computers? Can they use smartphones? What is their age? What are their motivations? What are their work conditions like? Are they highly-skilled surgeons or are you training a new computer analyst? And do either of those people have time to take your training? Surprisingly, I've had to deliver training to surgeons who didn't have any free time for training. All their time was dedicated to doing surgery or spent with patients. They simply told me that they didn't have one hour for a face to face government-mandated training course. As a result, I needed to come up with a solution that worked for them and our company's lawyers, which in the end was an eLearning solution. This is why the learner analysis is very important. Does the audience prefer a certain kind of training? Are they used to online courses? Are they more comfortable sitting in a classroom?

I've had to deliver training where not only did I have to teach the students the content in the training course, but I had to teach them how to turn on a computer, use a keyboard/mouse, etc. I'm not talking 30 years ago either this was in the 2000s when we had cell phones, internet, personal computers, and laptops. The point here is: Make sure you know who your learners are going to be so that your solution meets their needs.

Note: In a lot of texts, you'll see people discussing learning styles during the learner analysis. Remember, there's not a lot of research to support learning styles (as in none to show they actually exist), so we're not looking for that in our learner analysis. We might look at what the learner preference is, but those are not the same thing. There is no learning style. We might examine if the learners prefer and are used to learning via video, online learning, computer-based training, classroom, etc.

Next, we have our context analysis, which examines the kind of conditions where the learners will use their new skills. What kind of conditions will these learners be trained in? Are we going to teach them in computer labs? What are those computer labs like? What kind of technology is there? Are we doing this training online? If so, do they have a learning management system (LMS)? If so, what kind? This is where we answer the how? and where? What are the environments like? What technology is available? What's the budget like for that technology?

Many times I need to sit with the client and walk them through this part, especially a smaller company. The reason for this is that often a smaller company doesn't have an LMS and doesn't know what one is. Yes, they agree to want it when I explain what it is but they don't realize what goes into it, how much it costs, etc. You must have answers (at least estimates) to these questions when meeting with clients. They usually haven't thought this through so you need to be able to do that spontaneously. Often they believe you can sit down and 'just do training', and they haven't thought through all the preparation (analysis and design) that really goes into it. Many times I need to walk them through it step by step while we figure out what they want, how long it takes, how much it costs, and how quality can be impacted by deviating away from what I am recommending. Many times this happens during my initial meetings with a potential client. A larger company most likely (not always) has an LMS and they will want the training integrated with it. Thus context analysis is extremely important!

Gap analysis. Now you might be saying, I just did a gap analysis in my front-end analysis (FEA)? Yes, you may have and no, you may not need to do another, but there are differences between the gap analysis in the FEA and the one described in a needs analysis. The difference is that in FEA we were trying to determine if the problem was really a training problem. During the needs analysis, we already know training is a solution to that problem. This gap analysis is focusing on the best method to solve that training problem. Realistically on most projects, you are doing one gap analysis which confirms that training is the problem and helps us determine how to solve that problem. When I list out the steps as I am doing in this text, they are broken up purposely as two separate gap analyses because sometimes you are ONLY hired to do one of them (i.e., to do a front end analysis to determine if training, communications, etc. is the problem) and many times it may not be an instructional designer doing that front-end analysis but someone in process improvement, business architecture, etc. In that case, another one like this would need to be done because you need the correct information to determine how to best solve the training problem.

Table 2.0

Current State	Desired State	Recommended
What is the current state?	What does the client desire?	What is the optimal solution that meets the clients needs?

In the gap analysis, we are able to compare the current vs desired states (See table 2.0) to determine a solution that meets our client's needs (timeframe, budget, scope, and quality). The current state is the state of the company, team, and problem. The desired state is what they would like to have. The client might also have a dream desired state, which is unrealistic, so I might present them with multiple solutions, each with varying levels of complexity (i.e., bells and whistles). You do this because your client doesn't always have time or money for their desired state. Sometimes you have to present them these options. I also provide the proposed budget, timeline, and impacts for these options. How do each of these solutions really impact the company? What is the return on investment? For example, I might present them with four scenarios and ask which works within the time, budget, quality, scope. Which one of these do they really want? Then they can select which best meets their needs. At this point, the client must agree to a solution before you can start designing...but there is still more to be done in the analysis before I write my proposal and give them a budget so let's continue on before we get ahead of ourselves!

There is one additional thing I do here while I am doing my other analysis - a content walkthrough (brief content analysis). This is usually a short session where I sit with the SME and go through the client's content or it may even involve me looking at documents/materials. The goal is to determine how much content needs to be included in this training so I can come up with a budget/schedule. This is not task analysis (described later in this text). I do this because before I can give my client a solution, I really need to see what I am dealing with. Sometimes this is simply a quick 20-minute session with a SME who walks me through the content or system. This then gives me an idea of how long this training is going to be   something that is very important when giving my client a price for this training. I find that clients have a lot of trouble coming up with time estimates, they usually always underestimate. They may tell me they want a 30-minute computer-based training session but then after looking at the content I realize it's going to take 2 hours to cover their material. If I don't do this and I take their word for it my budget and schedule will be way off and they will not be happy. This content analysis is very important!

At this point, I have done my needs analysis. I should have a solution in mind for my client. I need to now write a goal statement and present a budget and schedule for that proposed solution.

There are two kinds of goals. The first one is a project goal (think project management goals), that is related to the overall project. For example, a sample goal might be: the project will be completed in budget or the project will be completed by quarter three of this year. Those are your project goals. You don't usually see them discussed in instructional design because they're project management related but if you're trying to be an instructional designer and you're going to be writing proposals; you have to write project goals and instructional goals. ID is so intertwined with project management that it's a mistake to not know both. They have to be taught together in unison like this.

The other type of goals are our instructional goals. These are our goals for instruction. These are not specific, they are not objectives. They are what you're going to do for the project. For example - Train users to fly a plane; train trainers to use the new computer software for accounting, etc. These get broken down further when we start our goal/task analysis, which I usually begin right after this phase after the client approves my project!

Additionally, when I talk about goals, I like to mention the term objectives so that I can explain the difference between these two terms. I think it needs to be very clear. A goal is not specific. It's very general, abstract. It's not an objective.

An objective is very specific and measurable - easily measurable. A goal can be measurable too but they are generally more subjective. For example, the goal – 'Fly a plane', is not specific. It's not broken down into specific tasks.

To illustrate this in another example - my goal is that the learner will be able to perform a needs analysis. An objective for this goal could be, given xyz case scenario, the learner will be able to conduct a learner analysis. The objective is much more specific. I could even get even more specific. For example, the objective could be - Given a context analysis, the learner will be able to identify what the environment is. Those are objectives. **I can write many objectives based on that one goal.** Hopefully, that clears up the difference between those two. It's important to know if you are discussing a goal vs objective.

At this point in the process, we need to get approval/sign off. If I am the consultant I would write a proposal and get the contract signed. Otherwise, I would get the project approved by my sponsor so that I could continue to design. Once the project is approved I move onto the next phases. This may have seemed like a lot - and it is. The interesting part is that most of the time I can do all of this - Front-end analysis, learner analysis, context analysis, and gap analysis in just a few meetings with a client. With experience, you learn how to make the most of those short meetings to get the information you need to solve the client's problem and write a good proposal.

4.1 Task Analysis

Once we have received approval to move forward with our project, we're ready for our task analysis. This means you're ready to break those project goals down into skills and knowledge so that you can make sure that you know exactly what the learners need to know. This analysis is the part of the process where we gather and organize all of the content.

The reason we perform this task analysis is because you need to know what they, the learners, need to know before you start designing any type of training; how could you put together training if you weren't 100% sure what content needed to be delivered? After we get all of the content from our Subject Matter Experts (SMEs) and organize it, we're ready to start creating our learning objectives and designing our assessments. If we fail at this, you can be sure that your training is not going to meet your instructional goals no matter how pretty your graphics are. Task analysis is not difficult to complete but it needs to be done correctly to ensure quality.

Tip - During this task analysis, I usually start working on some development (i.e. developing a template)

Tip – once you are done with your task analysis, make sure your SMEs and/or client sign off on it. It needs to be quality checked. It needs to be signed off on so that we can start writing our learning objectives. More than likely, you will have to work with your SME to gather this content (assuming you aren't the SME).

Breaking down your goals may seem very difficult at first and I think the hardest part of a task analysis is knowing when to stop breaking them down - how far must I dig? I see a lot of confusion on task analysis on the web and in texts. It's actually very simple. In the most simple terms, you are making sure you know all of the steps (or tasks) learners must know to accomplish their goals.

To gather this information, we may need to talk to our clients, do observations, document analysis, work with a SME, do interviews, or conduct surveys. Keep in mind if your SME is not available, you are going to run into a project hold up here. Be sure the SME and PM know what resources you need here because a SME that is not available will increase project time.

Steps to completing the task analysis:

I start by breaking up my high-level goals - what are the main things the learner's going to be doing for this goal?

For example, let's say one of our goals is for the learner to fly a plane. What do they really need to know? They need to know how to start a plane. They need to know how to steer a plane. They need to know how to read the instruments. They need to know how to eject in case of an emergency. And they need to know how to land a plane and take off. I have this high-level list of all of the things the learner needs to do to fly a plane.

Once I have those high-level tasks, I prioritize them. I usually put them into a table and I rate them with my client. I rate on a 1 through 10 scale based on importance, length, difficulty, and cost (4 ratings for each item). The goal of this rating system is to find out if this goal is important; do the learners need to know this? How long will it take to train someone to do this? Is this a hard cognitive task and will it be difficult to actually train someone to do it? How long will it take to train this task? How much will it cost to train someone to do this task? This breakdown helps my client to see the big picture and helps them understand how the instructional process works. This is also great when there is a pressing need to roll out training fast (rapid design, which is discussed later in this text). As a result, I might decide to eliminate a task because it's not that important or we have limited time.

My table might look like this:

Table 3.0

Goal: Fly a plane				
Tasks	**Importance**	**Difficulty**	**Length**	**Cost**
Read instruments	10	1	10	1
Eject from plane	1	5	1	10

Tip – If you have not done a thorough analysis, you may run into problems at this point in the process because a lot of times, a client has a great idea, but they don't always know what they really want and they didn't give you enough time to do a proper analysis. Not only did they not know what they want, but they don't have the budget for what they really want/need yet they expect you to deliver it, and you might have promised you could based on false assumptions.

Once we get into the task analysis and really figure out what the client wants you may need to readjust the budget/timeline. Many times we have already formed a contract and now we may need to revise or we risk scope creep. This is not a good situation. This is why I MAKE SURE that I have done a proper analysis and at least looked at their materials and made sure it all fits with their solution. Once you break down the tasks and see what is required for this project, you find out that you are not able to fulfill what was promised - you are in trouble! Make sure you perform the content analysis I suggested early in the project and you will mostly eliminate this issue. But if you run into this case, and as a new ID, you will; start by prioritizing as I did in my table above. Because if I prioritize, I can say, OK, well, we only have X amount in the budget or X amount of time. We're going to do these five things. We're going to skip these two for now. Maybe we're going to do them in the second round, for example, do the first two tasks now, to get started, and we're going to come back to tasks three and four at a later date. That's why I like to prioritize and this scenario is what happens all of the time when you are forced to write a contract without being able to conduct a very thorough analysis - that thorough analysis would have given me time to work with the client to figure out what they really need and want. The quick analysis only gives me a glimpse and it's very easy to miss something since many times the client under/over estimates what needs to be done.

Now that I have the high-level tasks for each goal, I start to break down all of those tasks even further. Eventually, I get to the point where I've listed every single thing they could possibly need to do and maybe more. I keep breaking this content down into simple steps. This is where my learner analysis really becomes important because I need to know what do my learners really know? What is their prior knowledge? When can I stop breaking this down? Because I can break down the task of flying a plane to a micro-level where the learner will identify what a plane is but my learners probably already know that! Maybe I do need to break it down that far but that is the point -

you, your client, the SME, etc. will need to determine that stopping point.

For example, let's take a task that everyone will know - how to properly brush their teeth. Do I need to teach the learner what is toothpaste? What is a toothbrush? What are different types of toothbrushes? You need to ask, do I need to break it down that far? What is the exact content these learners need to know vs. their prior knowledge?

Here is a sample task analysis for brushing your teeth. Notice how I have every task required to brush your teeth listed in the task analysis. You must have all tasks you are going to have in your training in the task analysis:

Brushing your teeth

- 1.0 Put toothpaste on brush
    - 1.1 Open the toothpaste cap
        - 1.1.1 take of seal if new toothpaste
    - 1.2 Put toothpaste on toothbrush
- 2.0 Brushing
    - 2.1 Brush time
        - 2.1.1 Brush for 2 minutes
            - 2.1.1.1 Brush each quadrant for 30 seconds
    - 2.2 Pattern
- 3.0 Gargling
- 4.0 Selecting a proper toothbrush
- 5.0 Mouthwash
- 6.0 What is toothpaste
    - 6.1 How is toothpaste made

Once you have the content organized, as shown in the list above, we are ready to move on. However, notice in the above example the task analysis is written out in a list format. You can create the task analysis any way you want, preferably the way that makes sense for the project. Here is another example, this time it's in graphic format. This format can be easier to visualize and is great when there is a lot of data.

Figure 3.0: Sample Task Analysis

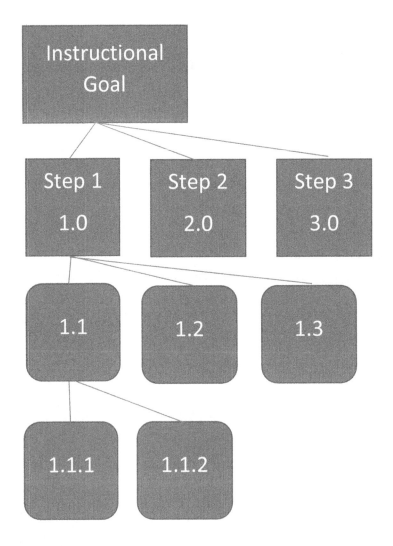

Once it's complete, we are ready for the client to sign off because there are going to be two things happening here. First, I am going to develop my analysis document (assuming the client wants one. I will always do this for large projects). Second, I am going to start working on my learning objectives and assessment items. So take pause and make sure your client or sponsor is prepared or ready for you to move forward. I keep adding quality checks like this in the ID process so that you don't run into scope creep later on. Scope creep means extra, new, or rework that the client adds which can hold up your project.

Let's assume my client wants me to write this up into an analysis document (mentioned in the previous paragraph) or I want to for my records, what does that document look like? Here's what you would include in a sample document to a client. One thing I will mention - my clients love getting this document even when they haven't asked for it. It shows them I am organized, on top of things, am going above and beyond, and know my stuff.

Analysis document:

The first thing that I have is I have a summary of the case - the training charter. Who's the client/company? What's the problem? What's the budget? What's my schedule? When am I having this done by?

Then we have the results of our gap analysis. We discuss how we collected data and what the results were. Describe the front-end analysis findings, the who, what, where, when, why are we doing this project.

Then we have a section for the learner analysis and context analysis - the results. We discuss how we collected data and what the results were.

Next, we write the project solution including our goals. Assuming we were able to do task analysis as part of this, I would present my high-level task list table with this document.

Design

5.0 Design – Learning Objectives

Hopefully, by now you have your task analysis completed and you are ready to write your objectives. **I usually do all of this (task analysis, objectives, assessment, and strategy) at the same time** but for a novice, I am presenting it in a logical order so you can see the big picture and see how each part is done correctly. See the example below to see what I create in this stage of the process. Essentially, I take each task and ensure that it's tied to a learning objective. This ensures that everything I need to teach is taught:

Table 4.0

Task	Objective
Order the steps for getting a law passed in the correct sequence (low-level)	Given a list of steps the learners will put them into the correct order with 100% accuracy.
Identify the capitals in the US (low-level)	Given a list of states, the learner will be able to state the capitals for each with 100% accuracy

Use coordinates to locate a global position (High-level)	Given coordinates, the learner will be able to identify a position on a map with 100% accuracy

Once I start analyzing my tasks and writing my objectives, I need to think about what kind of knowledge they are. This is important because I need to make sure the objective really meets my client's needs and is designed for optimal learning. For example, I need to know if my client just wants the learner to memorize random terms vs. being able to apply something to their job. Thus, I examine each task. Now the academic way of doing this is to examine each task and organize it via a learning taxonomy so let's talk a minute about them and I will discuss what I really do in practice:

While there are many different learning taxonomies - Bloom's, Gagne's, etc., I like to break my knowledge down into low/high levels. I have found that when designing, breaking it down further does not aid my instructional strategies. It actually ends up wasting my time. Low-level refers to factual information, such as recall, which "...can be remembered but cannot be used in new situations" (Mayer, 2014, p. 21). High level refers to problem-solving/transfer knowledge that is applied, used, and can be "organized into an integrated representation" (Mayer, 2014, p. 21). If it helps you to break it down further using a different taxonomy that is acceptable just make sure you find the method that works best for you and your team. Many instructional designers omit this step since you already have an order of content from your task analysis but I find this can be particularly useful when determining the strategies that I am going to use to present this content.

On the left-hand side of the table 4.0, you can see my first three tasks. On the right-hand side, I have the objective for the task. You can see in the first task, *Order the steps for getting a law passed in the correct sequence* that this is a low-level task. What I need to do is to write a learning objective that aligns, at the low-level, with that task. You can see in that table that my objective is, *given a list of steps the learners will put them into the correct order with 100% accuracy*. Thus, my objective is also written at a low-level. My objective isn't some problem-solving-level objective. It's aligned with the given task. This is very important. They need to be aligned or you start having quality issues with your instruction.

Now let's talk about how to write a proper objective. There are four key components that I like to see in an objective, usually referred to as ABCD.

If you look online, a text, or talk to other instructional designers, the ABCD method is very common. But some people have their own preferred method. But they all have the same basic information. ABCD - it's very easy to remember. What does that mean?

A - Audience
B - Behavior
C - Condition
D - Degree

Audience, Behavior, Condition, Degree (ABCD)

Let's go through it.

A is the Audience. Who are the people looking at this objective or taking this training? The audience. The learners, the managers, the admins, etc.

B is the Behavior. What are they actually going to do? This is where you write an action verb to define their action. Are they going to state something? Are they going to describe something? Are they going to evaluate something?

Tip - you can't use words like "understand" for this action verb. "Understand" is not a correct action verb. Why - because ask yourself what "understand" means. What does "understand" mean? I've asked several people in a class to write down their definition of "understand" and they all have a slightly different definition. In fact, they want to use the word "understand" in their definition. Go ahead and do it yourself. Try to define "understand." But if I say the word "identify," I'm very clear. That is a good verb to use to write an objective. The point being that your behavior needs to be clear and concise to match the task the learner is going to perform. The two worst offenders - the words "remember" and "understand".

C is the Condition. Under what conditions? For example, given a pencil and paper in a classroom, given a map, or using a calculator. What condition are they going to be able to complete this objective in?

D is the degree - how much success? 100% accuracy, 10% accuracy? What does success mean?

I have an example here, which is color-coded with each part of the objective.

Given a map of the United States, the learner will be able to identify the state of North Carolina with 100% accuracy.

Who's the audience? - the learner.

What's the behavior? Identify. The learner is going to identify the state of NC

What's the condition? Given a map of the United States. The learner is going to need to identify the state when given a map of the United States.

What is the degree? Success is 100% accuracy.

Some common mistakes I see people have when writing their objectives:

The first mistake is that people try to make the objective an assessment item. This is incorrect. You write your assessment next. The objective just tells us about the assessment item, it is not the assessment item itself.

Another common mistake is writing multiple objectives in one objective. Write only one. If you're writing multiple objectives in one objective, you're not using your task analysis or you didn't do your task analysis correctly. You need to go back and make sure those tasks are really broken down. Then write your objective. This means you should have one action verb. You shouldn't have multiple action verbs - just one per objective. An objective is one sentence, not 10 sentences. This is another error I see beginners make when they start writing a learning objective.

Here is a tip as you start becoming more familiar with objectives, and especially in practice - I don't write the audience (A of

ABCD), for every single objective unless there are multiple levels of learners/users (i.e., managers, employee, etc.) because usually, we know it's the learner. Additionally, if it's just going to be 100% accuracy for everything, I may not define the degree (D of ABCD) either. This helps me save time and reduce redundancy where it's not needed. It just depends on the situation. But I always have the behavior and the condition. And for those of you who are new, you should always have the audience and degree in there as well so you learn when to and when not to include them.

5.1 Instructional Congruency

This section is going to discuss the relationship between objectives and assessment items.

What is instructional congruency and why is it important for you? I already briefly described it in the previous section on objectives but I wanted to describe it here in more depth just to reiterate how important it is. Instructional congruency means that your objectives are in line with your content, which is then going to be in line with your assessment items, an idea, which is discussed throughout the ID literature (Dick, Carey, and Carey, 2014). In other words:

objectives = content = assessment

We are at the point where we have written our objectives which means you should know how we are going to present this content and how to assess it. Let's assume your objective is low-level knowledge, like verbal recall. This means that when I'm developing my content for that objective (my instructional strategy), that I will present to the learner, it needs to be presented in a manner that supports verbal recall. That also means when I develop my assessment, I'm assessing that objective at the verbal recall level. Everything should be in alignment. By doing this, we are ensuring that the content we present, and how we assess that content, is in line with our client's needs that we established when we did our task analysis and created our learning objectives. This is another quality check in the instructional design process. Take a look at the example below (Table 5.0). You can see that our original task was for the learner to identify the state of North Carolina. Then see that our objective describes that further by stating how that will take place. So we know when we are developing our content, we need to make sure the learner will be able to complete that objective (more on developing strategies later on in this text), and finally we can see our assessment tests that objective. Thus, instructional congruency.

Table 5.0

Task	Objective	Assessment
Identifies state of North Carolina	Given a map of the United States, the learner will identify the state of North Carolina with 100% accuracy	Please circle your response on the image provided [*learner is provided with a map of United States image*] Identify the state of North Carolina.

5.2 Assessments

As soon as I write an objective, I determine how it's going to be assessed, which should come directly from the objective (i.e., instructional congruency). I create my objectives, assessments, and instructional strategies at the same time. You must assess every single learning objective or you can't be sure the learners actually learned it! This section is going to overview assessments, describe several types, and provide you tips for developing them. Keep in mind this section is an overview of assessment design. I am going to provide some basic tips for writing assessments but there is much more involved than this simplified description. In fact, I teach an entire course on assessments exclusively and could write a book on only this specific topic, so keep that in mind as you read through.

First, I would like to talk about two types of 'evaluation' that must be discussed before we talk about the assessments that we do in ID and make it clear that there is a difference between evaluation and assessment. The assessments that I am referring to in this section are quizzes, tests, and surveys, which can play a role in evaluation. However, evaluation in ID is usually done to assess the effectiveness of something, like a course or program. Evaluation is discussed in a later section in this text. This section solely focuses on assessment.

Educators generally like to categorize assessment into two categories: Formative and Summative. Formative refers to interviews, observations, quizzes, homework assignments. It's an informal assessment. Summative assessments are final, like a final exam in a class, the SAT or other major test. A job interview could be considered a summative assessment.

I think it's important to understand the difference between these two because you need to know what you are designing an assessment for. Designing a simple class survey doesn't have the same implications that a test like the SAT can have.

Issues of validity and reliability become much more important when talking about high stakes tests. You should understand what reliability and validity mean because they can impact you if you are developing high stakes tests. I am going to simplify it for you to understand these two terms that many people use interchangeably (even though they shouldn't!)

Validity – Is the content in the questions correct? Are you using the test correctly? Those two questions are the key to validity.

If the questions are wrong or the content is wrong, you have weakened validity. If you aren't using the test correctly, it's not valid. For example, would a test requiring someone to carry 100 pounds be valid when the job requires you to type on a computer all day? Nope. It's not valid because they won't need to ever carry 100 pounds. You aren't testing correctly in that example. Now a test that required the user to type might be valid. This is the simplest way to think of validity.

Reliability – If the learners were to take this test again, would their score be similar to the first time?

Reliability is the ability for a test to provide similar results over and over. If person A scores a 5/10 the first time they take it, then 10/10 two days later even though they haven't studied anymore, the test is most likely not reliable.

What is the relationship between these two? Something can be reliable but not valid. Not the other way around. If something is not reliable, it cannot be valid. Let me provide an example - Let's say I know I weigh 200 pounds. If I step onto a new scale and it says I weigh 150 pounds, I know it's incorrect. If I step on that new scale 10 more times and it keeps saying I weigh 150 pounds. Guess what, the scale is reliable but not valid. It's reliably bad!

Pre- and Post- Assessments

The idea of pre- and post-assessments is an important consideration you may want to make. I am a big fan of pre-tests because they can tell you what your audience knows and how much they actually learn from your training intervention. For example, when I read a research study and they didn't use a pretest, I'm always baffled because the results are very difficult to make sense of because I can't tell if the intervention worked or if the participants already had the prior knowledge. This goes for corporate training too. In order to evaluate prior knowledge, there must be a pre-test.

That does not mean that the pre- and post-test need to be exactly the same. They can be different but of course, that means more time developing two different tests and developing tests is no easy task!

Let me demonstrate why this is important. If I develop a pre-test and on my post-test my learners improved by 80%, what does that tell me? It tells me my instructional intervention worked! It was a success! What if the improvement was only 5%? What does that tell me? It tells me that my instructional intervention either didn't work (assuming they scored low) or they already knew the content (assuming they scored high).

In practice, on most projects I am brought into I find we aren't testing learner's prior knowledge. But it's something I did want to bring up here, that pretest is extremely important and can tell us a lot about our training. When I am leading the project - a pre-test is mandatory!

Writing Assessments

There are many types of assessments and the goal of this section is not to list them all but to describe some of the most common ones and provide you with tips for developing them. I find instructional designers (and teachers) have a lot of problems writing assessment items. Why? Because they are hard to write. Especially when we start writing questions for high-level knowledge.

First, let's take a look at some common types of questions and types of knowledge they are good at assessing. Now please keep in mind this a guide, these are not hard fast rules. But these are the types of knowledge these questions routinely assess:

Table 6.0

Assessment Type	Low-level knowledge	High-level knowledge
True/False	x	(*not as common)
Matching	x	(*not as common)
Short Answer	x	(*not as common)
Multiple Choice	x	x
Performance	x	x

Notice how each type of assessment can measure each type of knowledge! That doesn't mean that it's the best choice, just that it can be done.

Tips for all questions. Keep in mind these are tips, not rules. If you have a reason why you would break one of these, go for it. The goal is that you do not want people who know the correct answer to get it incorrect because you wrote a bad question. We want to write clear and effective questions. Here are some tips for writing good questions:

- Make sure your answer is correct

- Ensure grammar is correct

- Don't use words like Always or Never because they are absolute

- If you have to use the word '**NOT**' make sure you highlight it in all caps, underline, or bold letters so that it is not misread

- Don't copy text/instruction from the content

- Make all incorrect answers plausible to someone that doesn't know the correct one

- Avoid patterns for answers (choose random)

- Avoid 'none of the above' or 'all of the above'

- Avoid 'which of the following are correct/not correct'

Types of Questions

True/false are very good at measuring low-level verbal knowledge. They can assess higher-level knowledge but there are better types of questions I would use instead. They are very easy to write and score. Unfortunately, the biggest disadvantage is that a learner might not know the answer but has a 50% chance of getting it correct. Questions with more than 2 potential answers are much less susceptible to this.

Multiple-Choice are good at being versatile, they are the Swiss Army knife of assessments. However, I often hear that multiple-choice are not able to measure problem-solving type of knowledge. They can actually do it really well. However, it's hard to write multiple-choice questions that are excellent and effective - it takes a lot of practice. They don't require learners to write, which makes them very easy to score. If I'm doing corporate training, I can assess a large group of people fairly quickly with multiple-choice via an LMS. It's probably the most popular type of assessment you see in education, corporate, and government because of these advantages.

Additionally, multiple-choice allows you to do a lot of different kinds of analysis on the questions. For example, item analysis (which is beyond the scope of what I am discussing here) is a great way to analyze these questions.

The biggest disadvantage is that learners can't apply their knowledge. They can't go above and beyond. There's no project. If poorly written, these questions can cause all kinds of issues, especially when you have questions that include "which of these is not" or "is the answer A, C, and B" and someone knows the answer, but they can't get it right because they misread the question or answers. Poorly written questions are very common mostly because it's difficult to write good ones.

Another big problem is that we mostly only write questions that assess factual knowledge. We're not addressing those higher levels because it is more difficult to write a multiple-choice question that addresses higher levels. Keeping to your objectives, as discussed in the previous section, will ensure this will not occur.

Another disadvantage is that learners can "guess". However, the statistics are more in favor of multiple-choice over true/false when guessing, which is why I much prefer them. On a question with 4 choices, someone has a 25% chance of getting it correct. The more questions you create, the more difficult it is, impossible even, to do well on a multiple-choice test if you're only guessing.

One may make educated guesses by using the process of elimination, which have a much greater chance than that 25% because they've eliminated one or two that they know definitely aren't the answer. But that's a different story than just pure guessing. Random guessing won't work on a test with 30 questions.

Short-Answer are generally used for verbal low-level questions. They're very easy to construct and they help eliminate random guessing. The biggest problem with them is that scoring is subjective. If you're assessing it on the computer via the LMS, which is typical, what happens if the answer is typed in all caps? Is it going to be recognized correctly? What if they misspell it? Is the computer going to recognize it as incorrect when you're not assessing spelling? You're assessing whether they knew the answer or not. Maybe they did know it, they just typed incorrectly. Should they really miss the question? Those are the kinds of things you need to consider when choosing short answer questions.

Performance (essay, case studies, problems, like ill- and well-structured problems, games, and simulations). These are great at assessing both low and high-level knowledge. The greatest advantage is that they can assess complex learning through real-world examples and/or projects.

They assess the ability to do high-level work. They're consistent with learning theory, like constructivism, where students learn through experience because they're going to need to demonstrate knowledge to get to the problem solution.

However, they can be difficult to create, which means they also can be difficult to assess. Scoring can be complex. A lot of people do not have the knowledge of how to develop a good rubric.

Let's take a look at rubrics. First look at the ineffective rubric. What would you consider in error in this rubric?

Bad rubric:

Table 7.0

	Great – 3 points	Ok – 2 points	Poor – 1 point
Written Expression	Supports main ideas with examples and uses	Somewhat supports main ideas with examples and uses at least some sources	Somewhat supports main ideas with examples and uses no sources

	several sources		
Spelling	No spelling errors	A few spelling errors	Quite a few spelling errors
Correct Length	Correct length – 3 pages	Almost the correct length	Very short work under 1 page

Usually, when I see a rubric like this I want to scream - and that is without reading it. Why? The first issue is that I see an even number of rows and columns. It's not that it's incorrect because of that but 99% of the time when you see that, it means it is wrong. What is incorrect about it?

Titles - What does 'Great' mean? 'Ok' mean? Or 'Poor' mean? Are those objective or subjective terms? They are subjective. Two different people might have two different takes on what each of those means.

Value - How important is written expression worth vs spelling? Based on this rubric they are both worth the same amount of points. But is spelling just as important as written expression? Was spelling part of the learning objectives or were we just assessing it now because we think it's important? We need to list the value for each item.

Objective - Is each description objective? That is, would 5 different people looking at the same paper score it exactly the same? No. Why? Take a look at the written expression for 2 and 3 points. What is the difference between the words 'several' and 'some'? There may be none. Additionally, that 2-point box for written expression is assessing two different things – 'examples' and 'sources'. What if they get one and not the other? Is it clearly defined how to break up those points?

Now let's examine what a better rubric looks like:

Table 8.0

	3 points	2 points	1 point
Use of examples (worth 75% of grade)	Supports each of the 5 main topics with an example	Supports at least 3 of the main topics with an example	Supports at least 1 of the main topics with an example

	2 points	1 point
Use of sources (worth 5% of grade)	Uses 2 or more sources	Uses 1 source

	3 points	2 points	1 point
Spelling (worth 10% of grade)	0 errors	1 error	2-5 errors

	3 points
Correct Length (worth 10% of grade)	3 pages

First, take a look at how the rubric is broken up into four different sections. This is done because some of the items didn't need the same exact number of columns. Next, look at the value. We see 'Use of examples' is worth 75% of the grade but 'Use of sources' is only worth 5%. This way we apply the correct value to each item.

The titles are simply points, this helps avoid confusion over what terms may mean to each scorer. Additionally, notice how each item in each box is objective - there is no argument over what is correct or not. This helps ensure multiple scorers score the same and that learners know if they are correct or not.

This is what a rubric should look like. It is effective and concise.

5.3 Instructional Strategies

While working on our task analysis, learning objectives, and assessment items, we also need to start thinking about instructional strategies. Just a note here - I am starting to plan these out from the first time I speak with my client. I am always thinking about my design. However, these become fully developed during my task analysis and objectives.

I find that one thing that a lot of new instructional designers get confused about is what are instructional strategies. I am not going to go through and explain every instructional strategy here because there are thousands; my goal is to show you how they are used so that you understand how to create quality instruction.

There are three types of instructional strategies - organizational, delivery, and development (Smith and Ragan, 2004). In this section, we are going to focus on organizational and delivery. Development will be discussed in the development section 6.5 of this text.

Organizational strategies are used to organize the course, lesson, presentation, etc. They're your skeleton, your outline. The most well-known organizational strategy is Gagne's 9 Events (Gagné, 1985).

While this is great for organizing my content, it doesn't really tell me how I am going to make my content fun, motivating, etc. Thus, it's a guide to help me organize my course. It doesn't matter if I'm doing a lecture, computer-based instruction, a video, etc. I must incorporate an organizational strategy like

Gagne's Nine Events (or parts of it that make sense for my project) into my instruction to help me structure and organize.

Next, I have my delivery instructional strategies. These are things that I use to design my content so that learners can learn and are motivated to learn. Some examples would include Keller's ARCS Model (Keller, 2009) (for motivation) or various learning strategies like problem-based learning, games, gamification, reading aloud, worksheets, drill and practice, etc. - they are too numerous to name. How do I determine what delivery strategy I need to use? I look at my content, consider my learners, and determine what is best and plausible given my project restraints.

What kind of project restraints? First, I need to consider the content - I look at my task analysis and objectives. Many times I know exactly how the content should be presented based on my tasks. But in addition to presenting it, the learners need to remember it! So I determine the domains of learning that I'm going to use for that content type. In Bloom's Taxonomy (Bloom et al. 1956), there are three domains of learning - cognitive, affective, and psychomotor. Cognitive is our mind, our thoughts, our knowledge, what is happening in our head as we think and learn. Affective is our emotions, attitudes, beliefs. Psychomotor are hands-on and physical skills.

The domain each task from my task analysis falls into will help determine the strategies I am going to use. For example, if my task involves being able to recall content, I know my instructional delivery strategy falls in the cognitive domain, thus I would want to use delivery strategies that support learning from that domain. Keep in mind one course may use many different strategies and hit on all 3 of the domains. Once we determine what domain my content falls under, I look at the knowledge type (high- or low-level) and look at strategies that support learning from that domain/knowledge level.

So how are these organizational and delivery strategies actually applied? How does this help you design? Let's examine the following:

In the table below I have two organizational strategies: Gagne's Nine Events and Dick and Carey's Instructional Strategies Model along with my general organizational strategy (Dick, Carey, and Carey, 2014; Gagné, 1985). My general strategy simplifies these organizational models so that it's easier to see the big picture and see how all of these organizational strategies are really saying the same exact thing.

The following are adapted from Dick, Carey, and Carey (2014) and Gagné (1985):

Table 9.0

General Organizational Strategy	Gagne's 9 Events	Dick and Carey
Introduction	Gaining Attention	Pre-Instructional activities
	Informing the learner of the objective	a. Gain attention/motivate
		b. Describe objectives
	Stimulating recall of prior knowledge	c. Recall prior knowledge

Content Presentation and Learning	Presenting Material	Content presentation a. Content b. Examples
	Providing learning guidance/facilitate	Learning participation a. Practice b. Feedback
	Eliciting performance	
	Provide Feedback	
Assessment	Assess Performance	Assessment a. Entry behavior test b. Pretest c. Posttest
Utilization	Enhance retention and transfer	Follow-through activities a. Memory aids for retention b. transfer

During the introduction (See Table 9.0) our goal is to get the learner ready to learn. We need to motivate them, tell them what they are going to learn, and recall any prior knowledge they may have. This sets the stage for the course they are going through.

Now that our learners are ready to learn it's time to deliver the content. The order of the content should have been determined by our task analysis and the strategies to get them to learn should be used here (i.e., problem-based learning, gaming, etc.). What are we going to do to get them to learn? How are we going to deliver the content? How are we going to ensure that our learners learn? Are we going to lecture? Have videos? Games? Case studies?

Our goal here is to teach the learner and have them learn using a strategy that matches our learning objectives. If the objective is low-level, like recall a name, use a strategy that supports that. If the objective is high-level, like solving a problem, use a strategy that supports that like problem-based learning. Your strategies should align with your objectives. This ensures that the learners are learning what they need to as identified in your task analysis. Keep in mind that the learners must know the content well enough to meet the desired learning objectives because they are going to be assessed on it! The assessment should be aligned with our learning objectives and should already be created per the previous section of this text (5.2).

And then finally, follow-through activities, which are memory aids for retention and transfer. This could include a job aid or how-to videos, follow up instruction, practice, mentorship, sandbox, etc. *Just a note - A sandbox system means a practice system. For example, if I was teaching someone how to use their new computer system i.e., a new learning management system, they could go in and practice without messing up the real system because it's on another server. A lot of companies will have a sandbox system when they're installing something so that people can practice using it before it's actually launched.*

The following table shows when in the organizational strategy various delivery strategies can be implemented:

Table 10.0

General Organizational Strategy	Delivery Strategy (How and where they fit into organizational strategies)
Introduction	Keller ARCS
Content Presentation and Learning	Problem-based learning Game-based learning Worked Examples Lecture Video Activities
Assessment	Tests Projects Assignments

Utilization	Job aids
	Apprenticeship
	mentorship
	Coaching
	Sandbox/simulation
	Drills

Now that we know our organizational and delivery strategies, it's time to start working on our deliverables!

Development

6.0 Common Deliverables

What kind of deliverables are instructional designers expected to create? There's a number of common deliverables that we create. It would be impossible to go through every deliverable you may ever encounter but the goal of this section is to explain some of the more common ones that you will be expected to develop. Project requirements and the type of training you are developing will help to define what deliverables you should be developing but this is a beneficial general guide for someone brand new and not sure what you develop as an ID.

keep in mind these are deliverables you usually create for the client. I am not discussing proposals and other PM/internal deliverables in this section

Instructor Guide

An instructor guide is a combination of the learner guide (described below) and the instructor notes. It includes everything the learner is going to do and see plus includes extra directions for the trainers. For example, if you were facilitating a train the trainer session, you would deliver an instructor guide as part of the training to the new trainers which would include PowerPoint slides, worksheets, activities, and notes.

What does an instructor guide look like? It's a guide for the teacher - a cookbook for delivery. It has all of the content and tells them when and how to present it. It's very detailed and has word for word directions. For example, it might be a printout of PPT slides with notes on the side of each slide telling the instructor what to say and how long to spend on each slide. In the beginning of the booklet, it might tell the instructor how to introduce the topics, include an ice breaker, and give directions for delivery. It goes through step 1, step 2, step 2, step 3. It's similar to a lesson plan that a teacher uses. For example, if you're going to be delivering training over an eight-hour day, this guide would contain the schedule and materials for those 8 hours. Here's everything you're going to **say** and **do**. Here's the presentation, handouts, and all materials. There is no one way to develop this guide, it's going to include what is needed for the training being delivered.

Learner Guide

Along with the instructor guide, we have a student or learner guide, which is usually a slimmed-down version of the instructor guide. In fact, it's nearly identical to the instructor guide except it doesn't contain all of the instructor notes. For example, it might include activities, worksheets, and all materials the learners will need. It does not include any instructor notes. Learner guides are very common in face-to-face instruction.

Presentations

These usually go with my instructor/learner guides. They can be printed on a slide per page, multiple slides per page, or simply be an electronic file. A suggestion - learn many types of software to develop presentations. Don't always rely on PowerPoint (PPT).

Computer-Based Training (game, simulation, software are included here as well)

For a computer-based training module or course, where there's no facilitator, you're not going to need an instructor guide. But now we are going to be delivering a stand-alone piece of content for the learners. This would include the files - both executable and development (if requested). It would include all narration, images, videos, etc. that were included in the development as well. I used to deliver these via CD/DVD but now I simply put them onto a cloud server or the clients LMS depending on their needs. Similarly, I would deliver the same things if I were developing a game or simulation.

Video

Video is a very common deliverable. We might be creating a bunch of vignettes, little short tutorials, or job aids. I've created large videos where I've had to work with a production company to create very large training videos and I've done small in-house videos as well. Creating quality video can get expensive fast and I personally like to hire a professional rather than attempt to do it all myself.

Narration

It's very tough to find someone with a really good (professional) voice. Usually, as an instructional designer, you're not necessarily doing the narration yourself, you're getting a professional to narrate. Remember, if you want to produce something with professional quality, hire a professional voice talent. As an instructional designer, you need to be able to produce it. Production includes learning how to take out breaths, how to instruct the talent to speak correctly, how to have the right tone and pitch, and then put it all together.

In recent years, a lot of text to speech programs have made their way into the market. I have tested these extensively and none are nearly as effective as a human voice. They often sound like a robot. I think they may be used for a word or sentence here or there but I would not deliver full narration to a client using one unless the client requested it. Hopefully, these will become better in the near future as I think they have a lot of potential. If you are looking at this after the date of publication there may very well be a good option out there.

Job Aids

A lot of times we'll be expected to develop job aids, which are simple tutorials designed to jog someone's memory while on the job, especially if there is a lag in between training and use. These can be developed many different ways: video, word document, etc.

Images

You will be using images quite often, regardless of the types of training you are developing. One recommendation I have for all instructional designers - purchase a gallery of images online that you can keep using. There are tons of great images online and they are relatively inexpensive. Subscribing to just one or two can have you covered for most image needs. Otherwise, you need a graphic designer or you need to design them yourself.

Other materials

Along with the materials described above, there will always be a need for additional items depending on the learning outcomes, client, students, environment, etc. So be prepared to develop other materials as needed. For example, for instructor-led training there may be a need to hand out worksheets. For computer-based training, there may be a need to have some supplemental materials. There may be a need to recommend an LMS and help with installation, etc. There are many reasons you may need to develop this extra material so be prepared to do it when needed.

Chart highlighting training deliverables:

This chart is a very general guide showing the types of deliverables based on the type of training being delivered. For example, for face to face training, you probably need an instructor guide (assuming it's train the trainer), a student guide, possibly videos, job aids, and other materials.

Table 11.0

	Instructor Guide	Student Guide	CBT	Video	Narration	Job Aids	Other materials
Face-to-Face	x	x		x		x	x
Online learning			x	x	x	x	x
Self-Paced			x	x	x	x	x
On the job			x	x	x	x	x

6.1 Storyboarding

Storyboarding is a sample of what our product is going to look like. For instance, if we were creating computer-based training (CBT), we would storyboard each screen so that our client could approve it before we develop it and/or so that we could hand it off to a developer. This is not something that needs to be done all of the time, for example, it probably doesn't get done for face-to-face instruction. But since most IDs tend to design computer-based training most of the time, it needs to be discussed because it does need to be done for computer-based training.

This happens in between or during design just before development. As soon as we have our solution, we can start deciding what the training will look like, so we storyboard.

Initially, the interface (prototype) can be designed while we are doing our task analysis but the actual storyboards (interface with content and strategy) cannot be developed until we have completed design. If you think about it, how could we develop a storyboard for something when we don't know what the objective is? Interface yes, storyboard, no.

While many IDs are one-stop shops (as in *you do it all*) you may be working with a graphic artist or programmer at this point to make sure what you are designing in your storyboards is feasible and works. Be sure you develop a style guide when beginning your storyboards to help with development (I discuss this in the next section of this text - 6.2).

One reason we create storyboards is so that our programmers can see what they are expected to develop (though most often we are developing it ourselves, it just depends on the project). But the most important reason you create them is that you want to make sure that your client signs off indicating that the project is 100% correct. You want to do this before you spend great amounts of time, energy, and money developing something you want to ensure its right. Think of storyboard as a quality checkpoint. You must get approval from the project sponsor before you start development. This ensures that you are not going to have to redevelop something based on an error you have made. Trust me, scope creep/redevelopment happens. Clients will change their mind. Getting a sign off here ensures you got approval to start development.

What information does a storyboard contain? How do I begin? It contains the content needed for the project you are working on. There is no magic format. I have seen several variations/formats of storyboards and they all worked just fine. The point is a storyboard does not need to be a professional piece of work. You probably hear stories of a storyboard for a movie that was drawn on a napkin in a bar. A storyboard can be very simple. I like to start my storyboards with a very simple drawing, usually done very early in the instructional process, possibly when I am presenting a solution to my client. I don't do all my storyboards like this, but my first one I will. I'll probably put two or three mock-ups together to show a client, and I draw them by hand.

This early hand-drawn process is called paper prototyping. It's when you draw it by hand, a real quick sketch of what it could possibly look like. Why do I do this? I do this for a number of reasons. One, I can draw so much faster than I can develop in PowerPoint, Word, Captivate, etc. to create a simple looking storyboard/template. This allows me to make changes on the fly and really brainstorm the look and feel with the client. I can sit with a client and draw several examples in minutes with them sitting there providing feedback as I go. I can create a sample in five minutes. I can ask them if they like this idea? Do they like where I'm going with this design? Do they want buttons at the top or bottom? I can draw with the client in real-time. It's a great way to get an interface sample very quickly.

You don't have to paper prototype. It's just something I personally prefer and I think is very helpful. A lot of times, I have an idea in my head and it's very easy for me to sketch it out and then work on it on the computer when the idea is more solidified.

What does a storyboard look like? As I mentioned already - a storyboard should include all the information that is required for development for your project and those requirements will differ by project. If you're not the developer, talk to your developer to make sure what you are proposing is feasible. I find most instructional designers do the development themselves so they are the designer and developer. The idea is you can take your storyboard, give it to a developer, and they can develop it. You've giving them the directions, the map. Figure 4.0 represents a sample blank storyboard that was developed in PPT.

Figure 4.0: Storyboard Sample

Per the example, you can see where you would put critical information like the file name, slide #, and any other identifying information that you may have.

On the left of the storyboard, we have our *files* section. Here you would be able to put all of the file names that would be used in the slide. Are you using images, what are the image file names? What are the button file names? What are the sound file names?

Then we have a *mockup of the screen*. This is very useful when you have a vision in mind and want the developer to get an idea what the screens should look like. I prefer to develop my storyboards with this visual though some designers just use an alt text with no mockup. I think using the mockup takes longer but does help with quality control, though either way is fine. Again there is no right way to do a storyboard. The right way is the way that works for the given project.

Notes for developer is a place for additional information that you may need to mention to the developer. For example, pause this slide at 1:00 minute in, etc. This is your chance to give the developer any potential information they may need for this specific slide. *Text/Narration* is an area where you may need to add the verbal part of the slide. I will put the actual text or narration that needs to be in the slide. Finally, *navigation and interactivity* is where I say what will happen and when. For example, the next button goes to slide 4. The back button goes to slide 2. There should be an invisible button or image that performs this action. There should be animation here.

There is no one format or one way it needs to be developed. The example I'm showing here is done in PowerPoint, but you can do a storyboard in anything. **Sometimes if I am trying to save time I will do my storyboard in the software I am developing in (this is a big tip).** This works great when I am the developer. For example, if I am developing in Captivate, I may create my storyboards in Captivate and rather than them being traditional storyboards, they may just contain the content, a skeleton of the final version without the actions but a perfect storyboard for the client to sign off on. This can save me development time. Doing this depends on a few things: Am I the developer? Do I have time for proper storyboards? And will the client be ok with this?

6.2 Style Guide

During prototyping and storyboarding, discussed in the previous section, you sit down with the developer(s) and SME and create a style guide for development. Why? Because we need to make sure what we want to develop is going to meet the technical limitations/standards of the client while retaining a high level of quality. **The point of the style guide is to define development styles. It's also very useful for a client when they need to edit the work at a later date!** This differs from storyboards because they define what each screen will look like whereas a style guide defines the styles I can and should be using for my storyboards. It also may contain micro information that is not needed on each storyboard.

What does it mean to create the style guide? It means I'm defining all styles (similar to CSS code for those that know a bit of programming). For example, I'm defining my fonts. Are we using Arial? Times New Roman? Just imagine how difficult it would be if me and five other people were designing or developing this and we all used a different font? Or we just didn't tell the developer what the font was going to look like and they chose one that the client didn't like? You can't afford that kind of rework. The style guide is a quality control document for development. I create it for all projects even when I am the designer and developer. This way when I go back to edit my training months or years later I know what styles to use.

Other styles in addition to fonts include colors for background, text, and anything else on the page. We define all colors. Usually, there's a color family, a list of three or five colors that work well together.

Screen resolution. Screen size. Are we creating this for a phone or a huge monitor? Because that makes a significant difference in our layout. Are we printing this or not printing this? How are images developed? Are we creating them in Illustrator or Photoshop?

What are we using for buttons (i.e., software? CSS?)? What do our buttons look like? Are we creating a template for them? What kind of spacing are we using? After a period (.), are we going to have one space or two spaces? What kind of white space are we going to have on the page in general?

Formatting. Are we using a style like APA for text? Are we going to have hidden data within each of these files? For example, SCORM or metadata? Are we going to have comments? Are we going to have developer notes hidden in the code?

We define all of this in the style guide. What you include is going to be dependent on your actual deliverables. But you need to have a style guide no matter what you're doing, whether you're developing a document, whether you're developing PowerPoint, something in Articulate, a game, etc. It doesn't really matter what you're developing. You always need to have some kind of style guide, even if you are the only developer.

Why? Because I've worked on projects where I develop it and guess what? The client comes back to me six months later and needs an edit. Can I actually remember what I was doing or do I have to go back and reverse engineer it to figure it out? The style guide saves me undue stress!

I personally always create a style guide. I was taught to do that from the start of my career, so I always have. But I've come into companies/projects where something was developed by a previous developer and there are no comments in the software, no style guide, no storyboards, no anything. In those cases I've wasted so much time trying to take it apart in ways it's not supposed to be taken apart, just to figure out what the developer did so that I can edit it. A style guide saves a lot of time. It's very quick and easy to do. It does not take a long time to create a style guide. You will benefit greatly by creating one.

6.3 What Types Of Software Do IDs Use?

This section will discuss much of the common software instructional designers use during development. Keep in mind this section is going to be outdated very fast. In just a few years this could be vastly different. Much of the software I learned years ago is no longer used today (Director, Authorware, Toolbook) though some of it still is (Photoshop, Dreamweaver, Captivate (Captivate was called Robodemo back then)).

What types of software do instructional designers use? It varies - We can end up using quite a few software packages for one project to very little, it all depends on the types of project we are on. I know a few IDs that only use one software program and that's it! Others use a different type of software for each project. It's going to vary quite a bit. What I'm going to do is describe some of the most popular basic types of software that we use and the types you should know before going into interviews. Obviously, this list is not an extensive or exclusive list. These are the main pieces of software I want to see on a consultant's resume. This is the software I expect my students to know. It's basic ID software!

I've broken this out into authoring, video, document organization, audio, image editing, programming, and learning management software.

Table 12.0

Authoring	Video	Audio	Document	Images	LMS	Programming
Captivate	Camtasia	Audacity	InDesign	Photoshop	Moodle	HTML and Dreamweaver
Articulate	Adobe Premiere	Audition	Acrobat	Illustrator	Any other	CSS
PowerPoint			MS Word			
Lectora	Final Cut					Design and Management (SQL)
	OBS					Javascript

Authoring software. There are two main big software packages, Articulate and Captivate. Articulate and Captivate. Articulate and Captivate. Articulate and Captivate. Articulate and Captivate. Yes, I repeat these on purpose because they are that popular. If you have never used Articulate and Captivate, think of PowerPoint on steroids.

Both of these are competing with each other – it's the biggest competition in our field, *which camp do you belong in?* I am asked this all of the time. I don't personally have a preference. They are both very similar in my opinion. I have both, use both, and teach both. However, one big disadvantage of Articulate is that it can only can be developed on Windows PCs. Captivate has the advantage that it runs on both a Mac and PC.

Most eLearning is created with one of these two pieces of software. There is other authoring software in the field that people are using, but these are the main two packages. So be sure to know one or both of these and include that on your resume and in your portfolio.

Having said that, there is a 3rd authoring software package that is often overlooked, which is PowerPoint. PowerPoint doesn't do nearly as much as either of those two pieces of software, but it can be used as a development tool, for lectures, or for presentations. I've seen it used for computer-based training and it does work really well in some cases. Don't be quick to dismiss PowerPoint, it can be very powerful and it's also great because your client can easily edit the file!

Video. There are three pieces of video software I think are important. One is Camtasia, which is used for screen recording and for making small quick videos. Next, we have more advanced software: Adobe Premiere and Final Cut Pro. Those are both a lot more advanced than Camtasia but I suggest learning one of them. They are designed for professional video and while I don't think you need to master them you should know what they can do and when to use them. I would expect someone making professional video to use one of these pieces of software. Finally, I would recommend learning OBS. OBS is an open-source software used for streaming videos to Twitch and Youtube.

For **document design,** we most often will use Adobe InDesign. We use this to make our instructor guides, workbooks, etc. We need to know Microsoft Word to develop documents. Pay attention to and learn the settings for formatting so that you can quickly make documents you are sending to clients look nice. Finally, you need to know Adobe Acrobat, which is used to create and edit PDFs. I also prefer Acrobat because I can sign documents for clients and get them paperwork very fast. This saves a lot of printing and mailing problems.

Audio narration. I strongly suggest Audacity. There's a lot of professional audio software out there, but I just can't find a reason to use anything else but Audacity. It's free and it's open-source. Adobe Audition is nice too but I find it cumbersome compared to Audacity.

Image editing. Adobe Photoshop for editing jpegs/pngs and Adobe Illustrator for creating logos. Image editing is a very important skill an ID should have. You don't need to be an artist or a graphic designer but you need to be able to edit basic images.

Learning management systems (LMS). You need to understand how to develop in a learning management system as well as manage it. It's pretty easy as they are user friendly and the great thing about learning one LMS is that the rest are all pretty much the same. So learn one, learn them all! The most common you see in highered are Moodle, Blackboard, and Canvas. But every company I've been at, every company I work with, every school I work with has their own. Some have proprietary ones and others have out of the box solutions. But they all basically function the same. It's sort of like email – you might have several different email carriers, for example, Gmail and Outlook, but they both send and receive email. LMSs are no different. They all have a slightly different development interface but function the same.

That is a pretty basic list for an instructional designer. I think this would be an excellent starting point for someone looking to improve their tech skills and develop their portfolio.

I didn't speak about hardware here and I'm not talking about programming. Instructional designers don't do a lot of programming. But we do dabble in HTML, HTML5, CSS, and JavaScript. We don't really get into database languages or things like that unless we're really getting into development. That's more computer science, not instructional design. I love coding but we just don't do it enough in ID. I do recommend dedicating some time to learn basic programming logic and some HTML/CSS but going above that isn't going to help you the way that learning Articulate and Captivate will.

6.4 Development Strategies - Theories Behind Multimedia Development

What is multimedia? We define multimedia as a combination of both verbal (words) and nonverbal images (Mayer, 2014). Verbal refers to audio narration and/or text. Non-verbal refers to images, graphs, charts, icons.

It's important for us to understand this definition so that when we speak to our clients we are able to communicate what we mean. For example, I have sat in groups and asked *what is the definition of multimedia?* And guess what? Everyone is very silent and finally, one brave soul will raise their hand and they'll say "radio, or newspaper", or a type of multimedia, rather than defining the term itself. It's not that they're incorrect, we all use terms like this, but we all have slightly different definitions. Always make sure you and the client have the same operational definition for terms like this so they know what you are talking about when you tell them you are developing 'multimedia'.

From this definition, the multimedia principle was developed by Mayer and colleagues, which has found that we learn best from text and images vs text alone (Mayer 2014).

But this multimedia principle is not new, It's been written and discussed since the 1960s when we were only able to test the theories on paper. It wasn't until the 1990s, when graphics were improved enough for learning enough for learning, that we could test them on the computer.

The background theoretical framework of this theory is that our working memory can only work with or process a few units of information at one time. This idea comes from Miller (1956), who theorized that humans could hold 7 units in our working memory at one time, depending on how interesting they were to us. We now know that number is probably closer to 5. Either way, we know we have a limited capacity to work with a limited number of concepts at one time before we start overloading our brains!

The application to practice here is that when I'm presenting a learner with some type of content, I can present them with a few concepts at one time before I need to get them to remember or discard them. If I try to give them 12 concepts at one time, we're going to overload their working memory.

Imagine pouring water into a glass. The water represents content and the glass represents our memory. The more this glass fills up, the more strain we put on our cognitive resources. The heavier the glass gets, eventually what happens? We get to the top of the glass and it overflows. Water is all dumped, spilling everywhere. Our memory is no different than that glass of water. It's how we remember.

We can only fill our memory up with so much information before we need to use strategies that allow our learners to remember it. So when you're doing a presentation, computer-based training, or video etc., you have to remember that if you're trying to get learners to remember something, you have to reinforce it and get them to remember it, before moving on to new things, or it's gone (i.e., you need to follow organizational and delivery strategies mentioned in the previous sections of this text).

Why is this important? Because we want to find the best possible way to deliver content to learners so they actually remember it. This is what IDs are paid to do!

6.5 Development Strategies - Multimedia Development

From the idea that words *and* pictures are better for learning than just words alone, Mayer and Colleagues (2014) came up with principles called the multimedia principles.

Before I list these, I want to caution you, take these with a grain of salt. We have research that shows that words and pictures are better for learning than just words alone. I did a meta-analysis on this and I found that it's about 12% better for both recall and problem-solving knowledge (Pastore, Briskin, and Asino, 2016). However, that is dependent on many variables, for example, how motivated your learners are.

One thing I do want to point out, very little of this research has tested these theories in real-life settings. Most often they were tested in very controlled environments with university or K-12 students. Do what's best for your learners, but know these and make sure you consider them.

Table 13.0

Principle	Description
Multimedia Principle	Presenting words and images that explain for one another are better than just words alone
Split Attention Principle	Text with images causes users to split their attention between them, causing them to go back and forth between the two to learn the concept. This increases cognitive load.
Modality Principle	Presenting narration and images allows learners to focus on the images and hear the words, reducing load vs images and text.
Redundancy Principle	Presenting redundant text and narration on the screen decreases learning and increases cognitive load
Coherence Principle	Extra details inhibit learning
Spatial and temporal contiguity	Text and images that explain for one another should be close together in both time and space
Signaling Principle	Adding signals, cues, bold text, highlighted words, etc. can help the learners identify important pieces of content
Interactivity Principle	Allow learners to control the pace of their learning

Table's content is adapted from Mayer (2014)

Look at each of these principles and consider them when you are designing your storyboards or developing your content. Which ones can you implement? In addition to these principles, we must consider usability in our designs!

6.6 Development Strategies - Usability

In this section, I will list some basic guidelines for usability when designing multimedia or web-based training. I do recommend following any of the number of course or training quality checklists out there when developing instruction. There are many out there depending on the type of content you are developing. The following are usability guidelines that should be considered for each project but please note this is just a sample and not meant to be an exhaustive list. Any quality checklist out there is going to be more comprehensive and focus on the specific type of training you are trying to conduct:

*Make dialogue simple and natural. Speak the user's language. This is very important, especially if you are trying to develop training for another culture, different levels of learners, etc.

*Minimize cognitive load. That's how many concepts I'm trying to get a learner to work with at one time. When I teach several concepts, I must provide an opportunity for the learners to learn it before moving onto the next topic.

*Consider the multimedia principles (see previous section on multimedia 6.5)

*No busy backgrounds; Background should not overtake text

*Buttons should be the correct size and easy to find (Fitts' Law). For example, a button that is too small on a mobile device might not be easy to press.

*Be consistent. For example, don't have a blue theme on one page, a green theme on another page, and a red theme on the next page unless you have a specific reason for doing that.

*Colors. Two to four colors is more than enough.

*Fonts should be legible. No unusual fonts unless you can justify it.

*Text should be clear and easy to read

*Layout should be very organized.

*Make sure that there is feedback throughout the instruction. For example, I might have a little note at the top of the screen that says you're on page 2 of 20.

*Clearly marked exits should be everywhere.

*Deal with errors in a positive and helpful manner.

*Always develop for the technology that your users are going to be using.

*Always consider the rule of thirds. The rule of thirds deals with placement on the screen. Imagine a tic-tac-toe board placed on your screen. The rule of thirds says that images should be placed along the lines and connecting points rather than smack dab in the center.

*Always provide help documentation.

6.7 Pilot Testing Software

If one of your deliverables for a project is to create some type of software (i.e., eLearning, computer-based training, video, etc), you have to make sure that it's actually going to work right on the end-users systems.

How do you do this? How do you test an executable file? What are the phases? What is the process for doing this? I like to do a number of things.

I have two phases in development where I test and retest my software. They are alpha and beta phases.

During alpha testing, I'm going to look for big, major problems. I actually start this step before I sign a contract with the client to ensure things are going to work as I promised. For example, if we've agreed upon a software to only find out that the client didn't really give me the right information about their back-end system. Then there could be significant problems.

I know to go and check that before I start anything. But they don't always know your terminology, and they may say they have an LMS or another term, but many times they aren't experts in this area and you need to actually confirm what they are telling you is correct.

Once I know it works, I start to stress the system. What does stress test mean? If I'm installing on a server or LMS, I make sure that works. Then, I develop a few screens, a mock up, a video, etc. and test away. I make sure it runs on the hardware and software my clients need it to run on. This way I can be sure before I get to develop that what I am developing is really going to run correctly on their system.

Next, I perform beta testing. Beta testing is done when I already have a developed product and am nearing or at completion. Here we're looking for little glitches and errors. For example, a link isn't working. There is a spelling mistake, etc. Very small minor details.

During beta testing, I start to involve the users. Usually, the way I do that is I'll start with one or even a small group and walk through with them. Here I can observe them while they're going through and I can fix all of the errors. I may do more testing depending on the scale of the training and number of problems I encounter but usually, one small group test is enough. Once I feel my software is complete it's time for implementation!

7.0 Implementation

The following section will describe the implementation phase in Instructional Design. If you recall from previous sections, the ADDIE process isn't linear, so implementation takes place throughout the entire process. Additionally, there may be different parts of the project that can be implemented at various times depending on your deliverables and client needs.

The basic premise of implementation is that I've delivered my product to the client and it's being rolled out to their users. I've developed it and handed it off. It is done (hopefully for your sake). Many times this is where my job as an ID stops. I hand off the project and that's it. However, sometimes I am responsible for implementation.

Regardless, one of the first things I do during implementation is to create a lessons-learned document. This describes what I have learned during the project thus far. It also includes any special notes about the client or project. This is very useful if I need to come back to the project or client in the future.

Assuming that I am responsible for more than just handing this off to the client, then there are many other practices I have to do to ensure my implementation goes smoothly. This could involve installing the software on an LMS, setting up the LMS, doing a train the trainer session, etc.

Many times, if they have an LMS, I may have to install the software for them on the LMS. For example, I may have to add a link in the LMS or even set up a course shell for them to teach the course. If I'm lucky they will have an LMS administrator and I don't have to do that. But you need to know how to do that so that you can have that as an option, This can make life much easier for both you and your client.

Another necessity may be to train-the-trainer (TTT). Train-the-trainer sessions can mean many things. Am I training a trainer to train all of the trainers? Am I training many trainers to deliver courses? Am I training trainers to be subject matter experts? There are times when you might even be the trainer, training the end-user.

Next, we need to consider change management and communication. If there is a significant change, I may need to help ensure that it's being managed correctly. For example, this might involve implementing a change model, such as ADKAR (change models are beyond the scope of this text). This is why an ID needs to ensure they understand the change process so that they can identify when it's needed and can walk the client through it.

Communication is usually part of the change process and implementation. Are stakeholders aware of the training and its impacts? Who is responsible for ensuring they have that information? I have worked with clients who have a communication team and others where I was expected to do it myself.

A final note here, as you are doing implementation, you need to be thinking ahead - to evaluation. Are you collecting the appropriate data for evaluation? This is described in the next section but be aware that you need to know what type of evaluation the client might want to do so that you can collect that data during implementation.

Remember, a poor implementation can make the greatest training seem terrible. You have to make sure that implementation is done well and it's smooth, successful, and error-free.

8.0 Evaluation

The following section will discuss evaluation as it relates to Instructional Design. There are a number of reasons why an instructional designer needs to know how to do an evaluation (*note we are not talking about assessments for objectives in this section*). Those can include something as simple as a quality check to something difficult like trying to determine if a project's return on investment was met. We could be evaluating a course or a program's success. We can evaluate lots of different things.

The two types of evaluation that IDs focus on are formative and summative. Formative evaluation is a small, simple evaluation, like a review or pilot test.

In the instructional design process, we use these to assess our quality, for example, I might have a subject matter expert review my design. These types of formative evaluations are consistently happening during many parts of the ID process. If you paid attention in my other sections within this text I point out when and what is a quality check!

Next, we have summative evaluations. Summative is the final evaluation. For example, determining the ROI, determining if students learned, etc.

The difference between formative and summative is fairly easy to understand. Formative is rather simple (i.e., quality check) and summative is more final (high-stakes).

When conducting a summative evaluation we first need to determine why we are going to do it. What is the purpose of the evaluation? From this purpose, we develop key questions which help to guide the rest of the evaluation. These key questions are the 'what' we seek to gain/learn/get from this evaluation. There can be one question or many depending on what we want to find out! Once we have our key questions we can select an evaluation model. The model we choose should be the model that best helps us answer our questions.

Most often this is Kirkpatrick's model. When I say it's used most often, it's used over 99% of the time (yes I made up that 99% statistic but I have rarely seen an alternative being used). Kirkpatrick's model is a buzzword within the field. If you're going to learn one evaluation model in our field, this is the one you're going to learn because it's hands down the most popular. It does a good job of addressing the impact of training courses, programs, and products so it's really good for use in our field for a number of reasons.

Having said that, let's talk about Kirkpatrick's model. There are four levels to Kirkpatrick's model (Kirkpatrick, 1994):

Table 14.0

Kirkpatrick's model
Level 1 – Learner satisfaction
Level 2 – Learning
Level 3 – Transfer to job
Level 4 – Return on investment

Level 1 is learner satisfaction. Did the learners enjoy the training? Did they like it? What did they dislike? Our goal here is to determine if the learners were happy with the training and what they believe could be improved. While learner satisfaction isn't always important (i.e. certain types of strenuous training) the data it provides can help inform the instructors, clients, developers, etc. what can be improved in the future.

Level 2 is learning. Did learning occur and if so, by how much? Thus in order to perform that measurement, it's beneficial to offer a pre- and post-test so that you can compare the results. **Keep in mind that learner satisfaction is not necessarily correlated with learning.** So you can have satisfied learners that didn't learn anything and vice versa. This is why you must measure learning to be sure. Additionally, this helps determine training effectiveness and can be used to help support levels 3 and 4.

Levels 3 and 4 are more difficult to capture and as a result not performed as often in most organizations.

Level 3 is transfer of behavior. Are the learners doing what they learned on the job? To collect this data you may need to observe behavior, analyze performance data, interview employees, and/or distribute surveys. This can be done at any future point after the training, 1 month, 6 months, or a year - it's going to be up to the client. I cannot recommend a timeframe because the project goals and client needs should indicate when this could happen.

Level 4 looks at the impacts. What was the return on investment? Before we start the training project, we always figure out what we believe the return on investment of this project is going to be; some kind of performance metric that we can objectively measure. Then we try to assess if this occurred.

This would depend on the project goals, for example, less errors in assembly, money savings, more productivity, etc. It's going to depend on the project.

If we were writing an evaluation report out for a client it would be organized similar to the following:

1. Background/Client

2. Stakeholders

3. Key Questions

4. Model selected

5. Data collection and Findings

6. Recommendations based on findings

9.0 Rapid ID: What, When, and How

Rapid instructional design. What does that mean? Why do we do it?

Rapid ID is designed for those that are experienced IDers, which is why I put this section at the end! For new instructional designers, we like to explain the ID model as linear with no room for modification (as I have explained earlier). These new IDers usually learn the term ADDIE, and they learn it as this very linear process, which confuses a lot of people because, sometimes, when they get out there in the field, they think that it has to be this linear model, which is not the case whatsoever as I've explained in previous sections of this text.

Here is a summary list of when/how you can do rapid design and/or cut time from the instructional process. Additionally, throughout this entire text I have given tips for cutting time:

1. Analysis is completed – without a proper analysis the project will fail. 70% of projects fail and poor analysis and management are usually the cause. This doesn't mean analysis always needs to be completed for every single project. For example, you might know these clients and have done other projects with them so you can take some/all of that original analysis and use it.
2. Constant access to SMEs, Developers, and Graphic Artists (and person who signs off – i.e., client)
3. Project can be rolled out in sections – for instance, one module can be rolled out by itself without the other 10 modules
4. Already have learning objects from other projects that can be reused and repurposed for current modules
5. Very limited interactions, graphics, and instructional strategies

6. Use easy to develop software such as Articulate, Captivate, or PowerPoint

The point of this section is to teach you how to take the ADDIE process and make it faster. How do we change the framework? How do we change the process of analysis or design? And can we change all those processes? That's really the big question, right? Can we change each of these processes?

Initially, we should discuss cutting project time. The easiest thing to do, the easiest time savings in instructional design, without changing the process at all, is changing your development tool (authoring tool). Why do I think that's the easiest thing to do?

Well, using a tool like Captivate, Articulate, PowerPoint, or MS Word vs programming/game development is going to save a significant amount of time and money. Thus, the easiest way to cut time on a project that has to move quickly is to use a simple tool for development. This is important before we move forward.

Let's talk about modifying the process. How can we modify the instructional design process? Can we really modify ADDIE? Yes. For example, I can do analysis many, many different ways. But I still have to always know what the problem is and have a solution - right? I still need to know who is the client? No matter what happens or how I modify the analysis, I have to have the basic pieces of information. If I don't know the problem, I can't solve it. So no matter what, you can't change that. You've got to get the problem. You've got to come up with a solution. That cannot be changed.

An example where I can modify the analysis: Let's say I've been working with a client for a while. I know them. I know who the learners are. I've done a previous full analysis. I don't need to redo it now. I've already done analysis. So now, I've cut down ID time significantly because I do not need to redo an analysis. So this second project with this client will cost less and take less time.

Another example of cutting the analysis: Let's say that a client comes to me and they say, *here's what we need. We need this eLearning course developed. We need you to start immediately.* Okay, so there is no analysis. They've told me the problem. I have to take their word for it. I will always caution them that I really hope that this is the correct solution. I can't guarantee it's going to solve their problem if I have not done a complete analysis but sometimes you do need to take their word for it and do a project like this because you need the work! Just be aware that you may be developing training for the wrong problem because they got it wrong.

Design and development. This is the nuts and bolts of rapid design. There are many things you can do here to save time. Roll out sections as they are done, reuse content, and create skeleton courses that can be completed later.

If the training can be broken up into sections, can we roll out section 1 while we are working on section 2 and so on? This can allow us to implement pieces as we go so that training is happening and we won't need to sit on section 1 for twelve months while we finish all ten sections of a course.

If you can reuse content, you can cut down time significantly. It's one of the reasons that we have SCORM (the idea that we can reuse - *note SCORM discussion is beyond the scope of this text*). If I'm working with a client and I've already designed some training for them, I may not need to redesign a new look and feel, new graphics, etc. I may be able to reuse the course shell.

Making a skeleton version is probably my least favorite option, but I've done it when needed. A skeleton version means very little graphics, no video, no interactions, no instructional strategies, no knowledge checks, etc. It's a skeleton designed to get the content out there with the idea that it will be completed later.

Depending on the client's needs I may do some or all of this.

When doing rapid design we need to be careful that we aren't cutting important corners, that may impact the outcome. Using this type of strategy really depends on the project but it's become a very popular selling point in an age where time is of the essence. If you are going to implement this be sure to explain to your client the advantages and disadvantages so that they can better make a decision on this type of design.

10.0 References

Anderson, J.R. (1976). *Language, memory, and thought.* Hillsdale, NJ: Erlbaum.

Baddeley, A.D. (1986). *Working memory.* Oxford: Clarendon Press.

Bloom, B. S.; Engelhart, M. D.; Furst, E. J.; Hill, W. H.; Krathwohl, D. R. (1956). *Taxonomy of educational objectives: The classification of educational goals.* Handbook I: Cognitive domain. New York: David McKay Company.

Branson, R. K., Rayner, G. T., Cox, J. L., Furman, J. P., King, F. J., Hannum, W. H. (1975). Interservice procedures for instructional systems development. (5 vols.) (TRADOC Pam 350-30 NAVEDTRA 106A). Ft. Monroe, VA: U.S. Army Training and Doctrine Command, August 1975. (NTIS No. ADA 019 486 through ADA 019 490). Retrieved from https://apps.dtic.mil/dtic/tr/fulltext/u2/a019486.pdf

Dick, W., Carey, L., & Carey, J. (2014). *The Systematic Design of Instruction* (8th ed.). Pearson.

Dwyer, F. M. (1978). *Strategies for improving visual learning.* State College, PA: Learning Sources.

Gagné, R. M. (1985). The conditions of learning (4th ed.). New York: Holt, Rinehart & Winston.

Gagné, R.M. & Driscoll, M.P. (1988). *Essentials of learning for instruction* (2nd ed.). Englewood Cliffs, NJ: Prentice Hall, Inc.

Keller, J. M. (2009). *Motivational design for learning and performance: The ARCS model approach.* Springer Science & Business Media.

Kirkpatrick, D. L. (1994). Evaluating training programs: the four levels. San Francisco: Berrett-Koehler.

Mayer, R. E. (2014). The Cambridge handbook of multimedia learning. New York: Cambridge University Press.

Miller, G. (1956). The magical number seven, plus or minus two: Some limits on our capacity for processing information. *The psychological review*, 63, 81-97.

Morrison, G. R., Ross, S. M., & Kemp, J. E. (2001). Designing effective instruction, 3rd ed. New York: John Wiley.

Pastore, R., Briskin, J., Asino, T. (2016). The multimedia principle: A meta-analysis. *International Journal of Instructional Technology and Distance Learning. 13(11). 17-30.*

Serrat, Olivier (2017). "The Five Whys Technique". *Knowledge Solutions*. pp. 307–310.

Smith, P. L., & Ragan, T. J. (2004). *Instructional Design* (Third ed.). Hoboken, NJ: John Wiley & Sons, Inc.

Made in the USA
Monee, IL
25 June 2021